Civil Litigation and Dispute Resolution

Legal English Dictionary and Exercise Book

MICHAEL HOWARD

Civil Litigation and Dispute Resolution

ISBN: 1514275511
ISBN-13: 978-1514275511

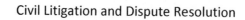

Civil Litigation and Dispute Resolution

Civil Litigation and Dispute Resolution

CONTENTS
Dictionary

Exercises

BUY MORE TITLES AT:

http://www.legalenglishbookstore.com

DICTIONARY

1 BEFORE A CLAIM

Adjudication (noun): This is a type of alternative dispute resolution commonly used in construction and building disputes. If there is a dispute over a building or construction contract, the contract will usually have a clause that requires the parties to attend adjudication proceedings before any litigation can be brought.
Associated Words: To Adjudicate (verb), Alternative Dispute Resolution (noun), Dispute (noun), Litigation (noun).

To Allege (verb): This verb is used in legal English when one person thinks that another person has done something wrong. For example, if Mr Jones thinks that Miss Davis crashed her car into his car, then he alleges that Miss Davis has committed the tort of negligence. Another way to say this is that he is "making an allegation against Miss Davis". It is important to remember that the tort (or crime) has not been proven in a court of law. It is only an opinion of a person's wrong doing or guilt at this stage. In criminal law you will also see the verb "to accuse" which has a similar meaning.
Associated Words: Alleged (past simple), Alleged (3rd form), Allegation (noun), To Make an Allegation Against Someone (collocation), Negligence (noun), Tort (noun).

Alternative Dispute Resolution "ADR" (noun): This is a common alternative to litigation. ADR has become more popular in recent years as it is seen as a faster, cheaper and more effective way to settle disputes without using the courts. Mediation is the most common form of ADR. It is also common for the court to order that the parties attempt to settle the case via ADR if possible before a trial is scheduled.

Associated Words: Case (noun), Dispute (noun), To Order (verb), To Settle (verb), Trial (noun).

Arbitration (noun): This is a process similar to litigation but with less formalities and legal procedure. The main aim of arbitration is to settle the dispute early. It is very common in international contracts and many standard contracts will have an arbitration clause. The clause will usually require all parties to attend arbitration before litigation proceedings are issued. There are specific rules for arbitration proceedings in England and Wales and it is becoming a useful alternative to court proceedings. There are also many conventions and institutions which govern international arbitration and, similarly, these are seen as a useful alternative to formal legal proceedings.
Associated Words: Contract law (noun), Dispute (noun), Litigation (noun), Proceedings (noun), To Settle (verb).

To Breach (verb): This is a very important word in civil litigation and dispute resolution. It means that someone has broken an agreement or has not done something that they should have done. It is commonly used in tort and in contract law, for example "breach of terms and conditions", "breach of obligations" or "breach of duty of care".
Associated Words: Breached (past simple), Breached (3rd form), Breach (noun), Duty of Care (noun), Litigation (noun), Obligations (noun).

Causation (noun): This is the connection between the defendant's breach and the loss suffered by the claimant. For instance, the tort of negligence requires that causation is established for the court to find in favour of the claimant. In other words the claimant must show that the acts or omissions of the defendant caused loss to the claimant.
Associated Words: To Cause (verb), Caused (past simple), Caused (3rd form), Claimant (noun), Defendant (noun), Loss (noun), Negligence (noun), To Omit (verb).

Carelessness (noun): Carelessness is a common English word that is used to describe the legal English term negligence. It means that somebody does not show enough concern or awareness about the possible consequences of their actions.

Associated Words: Careless (adjective), Negligence (noun).

Civil Procedure Rules (noun): These rules are commonly known as the CPR. They are the rules that must be followed in civil litigation cases in England and Wales. The rules were introduced in 1999 by Lord Woolf. The aim of the rules is to provide an easier, quicker and fairer system for all litigants. All lawyers who are involved in dispute resolution should be familiar with these rules in England and Wales.
Associated Words: Litigation (noun), Litigant (noun), Woolf Report (noun).

To Commit (verb): We use this verb when someone does something criminal or that is classed as a tort. For example, if someone steals something, we say that they have committed theft. If someone causes an accident, we say that they have committed negligence. To commit is used in both criminal law and civil law. It is not correct to say "to do/make theft" or "to do/make negligence". The correct verb to use is "to commit".
Associated Words: Committed (past simple), Committed (3rd form), Committed (adjective), Commission (noun), Negligence (noun), Tort (noun).

To Dispute (verb): This verb means to argue about something or to question something. It is used in legal English both as a verb and as a noun. The noun "dispute" is a situation when two or more people disagree about something. Civil litigation claims are also commonly called disputes.
Associated Words: Disputed (past simple), Disputed (3rd form), Dispute (noun), Disputed (adjective), Litigation (noun).

Duty of Care (noun): Under the law of tort an individual owes a duty of care to other individuals not to cause any damage or harm to them. This means that they need to be careful or responsible in certain situations. This concept came from common law and has developed over many years in the English courts. The duty of care is one part of establishing the tort of negligence. To establish whether there is a duty of care, the court will generally look at three things. First, was harm reasonably foreseeable. Second, were the claimant and defendant in close proximity, and third is it fair and reasonable to impose a duty of care on the defendant in this situation. If the situation satisfies these three conditions, the court is likely to conclude that a duty of care has arisen.

Associated Words: Claimant (noun), Common Law (noun), Defendant (noun), Foreseeable (noun), Negligence (noun), (noun), Tort (noun).

Foreseeable (adjective): This means that something is predictable or expected. The concept of whether an act or omission is foreseeable is an important concept of dispute resolution. Foreseeability is especially important in the areas of tort law and breach of contract. The court will look at foreseeability to help establish whether a defendant owes a claimant a duty of care and whether it was foreseeable that a defendant's acts or omissions caused loss or harm.

Associated Words: To Foresee (verb), Foresaw (past simple), Foreseen (3rd form), Foreseeability (noun), Breach of Contract (noun), Claimant (noun), Defendant (noun), Tort Law (noun).

Governing Law (noun): This is more informally known as the choice of law or applicable law. It is a very common issue in contract law. In legal English governing law means the country, state or jurisdiction where legal proceedings will be heard if the parties have a dispute. It is common for both parties to agree the governing law before executing a contract, however, it is also common for governing law to become a contentious matter if there is no clause in the contract or if the clause is not clear.

Associated Words: Applicable Law (noun), Contentious (adjective), Contract Law (noun), Dispute (noun), Jurisdiction (noun), Matter (noun), Party (noun).

Grounds (noun): This is the legal English word for the reason or the basis of a claim. For instance, you may often hear "what are the grounds for this claim?". This means, what are the reasons for the claim, or what happened to cause the claim. For example, Mr Smith sued the local supermarket for negligence on the grounds that they failed to clear water from the shop floor. Mr Smith slipped on the water and broke his arm. This means that the reason Mr Smith sued the supermarket was because they had failed to clear the water.

Associated Words: Claim (noun), To Sue (verb).

To Harm (verb): This verb means to damage or to hurt somebody or something. In civil litigation and dispute resolution it is important to establish or prove that the claimant has been harmed or has suffered loss.
Associated Words: Harmed (past simple), Harmed (3rd form), Harm (noun), Claimant (noun), Litigation (noun), Loss (noun), To Suffer (verb).

To Infringe (verb): This means the same as the verb "to breach", however it is only used in certain collocations and contexts. To infringe is usually used with human rights and intellectual property law. Common collocations in human rights law are to infringe freedom of speech, freedom of movement or freedom of religion. Common collocations in intellectual property law are to infringe copyright, trademarks or patents.
Associated Words: Infringed (past simple), Infringed (3rd form), Infringed (adjective), Infringement (noun), To Breach (verb), Copyright (noun), Human Rights (noun), Patent (noun), Trademark (noun).

Injured Party (noun): An injured party is an individual or organisation who has suffered harm or loss. In legal English the injured party is usually the claimant but it can also be the defendant, for instance in a counterclaim.
Associated Words: Claimant (noun), Counterclaim (noun), Defendant (noun), Harm (noun), Litigation (noun), Loss (noun).

Letter Before Action (noun): This is a letter sent from the claimant to the defendant before a claim is issued. The aim of this letter is to inform the defendant of the possibility of a claim and the details of the claimant's arguments. Due to the Civil Procedure Rules, it is usual practice for a letter before action to be sent before a claim is issued.
Associated Words: Civil Procedure Rules (noun), Claim (noun), Claimant (noun), Defendant (noun), To Issue (verb).

Litigation (noun): This means the process of contesting a dispute in the law courts. It is commonly used in civil law to describe the situation and procedure of a claim being issued by the claimant against the defendant.
Associated Words: Claimant (noun), Defendant (noun), Dispute (noun), To Issue (verb).

Loss (noun): Loss means that something or someone has suffered damage or harm. In order to bring an action in civil litigation the claimant must have suffered loss. Loss can be financial, physical or mental harm.
Associated Words: Claimant (noun), Harm (noun), Litigation (noun), To Suffer (verb).

To Omit (verb): This verb means that someone failed to do something that they should have done. In legal English, to omit is commonly used in relation to the tort of negligence, especially when considering a breach of a duty of care. A breach can be a negligent act or a negligent omission. A negligent omission is when a person does not do something and this causes another person to suffer harm. For example, if a building company fails to keep their building site safe, this is a negligent omission which may result in harm to an individual if they have an accident and hurt themselves. A negligent omission to act can lead to a claim in the civil courts.
Associated Words: Omitted (past simple), Omitted (3rd form), Omission (noun), To Breach (verb), To Cause (verb), Claim (noun), Duty of Care (noun), Harm (noun), Negligence (noun), To Suffer (verb), Tort (noun).

Overriding Objective (noun): The overriding objective is a principle from the Civil Procedure Rules. The purpose of the overriding objective is for the civil litigation and dispute resolution process to be fair, fast and inexpensive. The principle is that each case should be treated proportionally in relation to the size, importance and complexity of the claim and the financial situation of both parties. The court must consider the overriding objective when they make rulings, give directions and interpret the Civil Procedure Rules.
Associated Words: Civil Procedure Rules (noun), Litigation (noun).

Practice Direction (noun): These are the rules that support the Civil Procedure Rules. Each rule in the Civil Procedure Rules has a Practice Direction that provides further information on the rules.
Associated Words: Civil Procedure Rules (noun).

Pre-Action Protocol (noun): Some types of claims, for example personal injury and defamation claims, must follow a specific pre-action protocol.

This means that they have to follow special rules in the Civil Procedure Rules before issuing a claim. The pre-action protocols are designed to encourage openness and an early exchange of information to assist a negotiated settlement before the need for litigation. Under the pre-action protocols both parties must exchange information in relation to the dispute, open discussions for settlement and try to avoid bringing proceedings.

Associated Words: Civil Procedure Rules (noun), Defamation (noun), Dispute (noun), Litigation (noun), To Negotiate (verb), Personal Injury (noun), To Settle (verb).

To Resolve (verb): This word is similar in meaning to settle but it is usually used in the collocations "to resolve a dispute" or "to resolve a conflict". It means that an argument or disagreement is settled or agreed to end. Due to the nature of the Civil Procedure Rules the term "Dispute Resolution" has now become attached to Civil Litigation. Some law firms now refer to their litigation departments as dispute resolution departments.

Associated Words: Resolved (past simple), Resolved (3rd form), Resolution (noun), Conflict (noun), To Settle (verb).

To Settle (verb): This word means to resolve a dispute with the agreement of all the parties. It is a very important word in legal English as the concept of civil litigation changed with the Civil Procedure Rules. The emphasis of the Civil Procedure Rules is on settling claims and avoiding proceedings if possible. The collocation "to settle a claim" is very common in legal English.

Associated Words: Settled (past simple), Settled (3rd form), Settled (adjective), Settlement (noun), Claim (noun), Civil Procedure Rules (noun), Dispute (noun), Litigation (noun), Proceedings (noun), To Resolve (verb).

To Suffer (verb): This verb means to experience something negative. In legal English it is commonly used with harm, loss and damage. The phrases "to suffer harm", "to suffer loss" and "to suffer damage" are all collocations used in litigation to describe the claimant experiencing something negative because of the defendant's acts or omissions.

Associated Words: Suffered (past simple), Suffered (3rd form), Suffered (adjective), Suffering (noun), Claimant (noun), Defendant (noun), Harm (noun), Loss (noun), To Omit (verb).

Woolf Report (noun): This report produced the Civil Procedure Rules. The report, formally known as "The Access to Justice Report", was written in 1996 to help the individual's right to justice. In his report, Lord Woolf, a former barrister, recommended a number of ideas to help individuals achieve justice. For instance, the report says that the legal system should be fair, fast, inexpensive, understandable, effective and well organised.

Associated Words: Barrister (noun), Civil Procedure Rules (noun).

2 MAKING A CLAIM

Affidavit (noun): This Latin word means to declare an oath made in writing. An oath means a formal promise. The collocation to "swear an affidavit" is commonly used in legal English, however the recent movement away from legalese has caused the phrase to be replaced in the Civil Procedure Rules with "Statement of Truth". The word affidavit is still used in certain situations and in the US legal system.
Associated Words: Civil Procedure Rules (noun), Statement of Truth (noun).

Barrister (person): This is a type of lawyer in England and Wales. In the English legal system there are two types of lawyer. One type is called a solicitor and the other is called a barrister. A barrister will usually do the advocacy in a case after receiving instructions from the solicitor. Barristers are specifically trained in the skill of advocacy and legal procedure. They are famous for their court dress of long black gown and horse-hair wig and are also known as "members of the Bar".
Associated Words: Advocacy (noun), Solicitor (person).

To Brief (verb): This verb means to instruct. It is used in legal English when the client instructs or "briefs" a lawyer. To brief a lawyer means to give them information or instructions in relation to the case or claim. The word "brief" as a noun is sometimes used to describe a lawyer.
Associated Words: Briefed (past simple), Briefed (3rd form), Briefing (noun), Case (noun), Claim (noun), To Instruct (verb).

To Bring an Action (collocation): This means to issue proceedings. It is a common, formal phrase in legal English and can be used in a number of collocations, for example to bring a case or to bring a claim. It is also important to note that in legal English a claim is brought "against" someone. The full collocation would be "to bring an action against" (the defendant).

Associated Words: Brought an Action Against (past simple), Brought an Action Against (3rd form), Case (noun), Claim (noun), To Issue (verb).

Burden of Proof (noun): This means that one party has the obligation of proving their case in court. The burden of proof in civil litigation "rests" with the claimant. This means that the claimant must prove their case on the balance of probabilities. This means that they must show the court that their version of the facts is more likely than the defendant's version. The burden of proof in criminal law is defined differently and rests with the prosecution to prove their case so that the jury or judge is sure of the defendant's guilt.

Associated Words: Balance of Probabilities (noun), Claimant (noun), Defendant (noun), Obligation (noun).

Case (noun): This word is a general term that means matter or claim.

Associated Words: Claim (noun), Matter (noun).

To Claim (verb): In legal English this verb means to declare that somebody has harmed or injured you so that you deserve compensation for your loss. For example, Mr Smith claimed that Dr Roberts was negligent when he incorrectly diagnosed Mr Smith's medical condition and that this caused Mr Smith physical injury. The noun "claim" is also commonly used to describe a case or legal proceedings. The collocations "to make a claim" or "to bring a claim" are common in civil litigation.

Associated Words: Claimed (past simple), Claimed (3rd form), Claim (noun), Case (noun), To Harm, (verb).

Claimant (noun): This is the name of the party who issues a claim or proceedings.

Associated Words: Claim (noun), To Issue (verb).

Claim Form (noun): This is the name of a document used to issue a claim. The claim form contains the basic information on the parties, the grounds for the claim and the remedy. If the facts and grounds of the claim are complicated, the claimant can also file a longer version of the claim form called the particulars of claim.
Associated Words: Claim (noun), Claimant (noun), To Issue (verb), Grounds (noun), Particulars of Claim (noun), Parties (noun).

Court Fee (noun): This is an amount of money that the claimant must pay to the court when they issue the claim. The fee pays for the administration costs of the case.
Associated Words: Case (noun), Claim (noun), Claimant (noun), To Issue (verb).

Evidence (noun): This word means all the data and information used by the parties when they try to prove their case in court. Evidence can be produced in different ways, for example, it can be a written or oral witness statement, documents, objects, videos, phone records etc. Please note that evidence is an uncountable noun ("evidences" is not a word in English). To use evidence as a countable noun, the word "exhibits" can be used, especially for physical types of evidence.
Associated Words: Exhibit (noun), Witness Statement (noun).

Exhibit (noun): As stated above this word can be used in the same way as evidence but as a countable noun. It is usually used for physical types of evidence as stated above.
Associated Word: Evidence (noun).

To File (verb): This means to send or place with the court. Some common legal English collocations are "to file a claim" and "to file an application".
Associated Words: Filed (past simple), Filed (3rd form), To File a Claim (collocation), To File an Application (collocation).

To Issue (verb): The collocations "to issue a claim" and "to issue proceedings" are the formal legal English phrases that mean to start a claim or case in court. A claim is issued on the date the claim form is received by the court. The court will stamp the claim form to indicate that it has received all the correct documentation and the correct fee has been paid. After the court fee has been paid and the court has stamped the claim form, the claim has officially been issued.

Associated Words: Issued (past simple), Issued (3rd form), Issued (adjective), Claim Form (noun), To Issue a Claim (collocation), Fee (noun), To Issue Proceedings (collocation).

Issue (noun): This noun means a point or question that is in dispute.
Associated Word: Dispute (noun).

Limitation (noun): After the date of the defendant's breach (or the date that the breach was discovered), the claimant has a limited period of time to issue the claim form at the court. This is called the limitation period. If the claimant tries to issue a claim after the limitation period, the court may decide that the claim is "time-barred". If a claim is time-barred then the court will not hear the claim.
Associated Words: To Breach (verb), Claim (noun), Claimant (noun), Defendant (noun), To Hear (verb).

Litigant in Person (noun): This is an individual or organisation who represents themselves in court. They are not represented by a barrister or a solicitor.
Associated Words: Barrister (person), To Represent (verb), Solicitor (person).

Particulars of Claim (noun): This document is a longer version of the claim form that the claimant issues at court. The particulars of claim are for claims that are more complicated or need a more detailed explanation.
Associated Words: Claim (noun), Claimant (noun), Claim Form (noun), To Issue at Court (collocation).

Plaintiff (noun): This is the old legal English word for claimant. The Civil Procedure Rules changed this term. Plaintiff is still used in the US legal system.
Associated Words: Civil Procedure Rules (noun), Claimant (noun).

To Plead (verb): This verb means to declare or state your case or position to the court. The noun "pleading" is an old legal English word that means statement of case.

Associated Words: Pleaded (past simple), Pleaded (3rd form), Pleading (noun), Case (noun).

Proceedings (noun): This word has two main meanings in legal English. The first meaning is the ongoing process of a claim. For instance, "The proceedings have been unusually slow in this case". The second meaning of the word proceedings is the claim itself. For example, "Mr Pitt brought proceedings against Mrs Jones for breach of contract".

Associated Words: To Bring Proceedings (collocation), Breach of Contract (noun), Claim (noun).

To Serve (verb): This verb means to send or give documents to another party in the claim. It is a very important concept in civil litigation because there are very strict rules on how and in what time period documents must be served on the defendant(s). For example, after the claimant issues the claim with the court, the claimant must then serve the claim form on the defendant. The defendant must then serve the defence on the claimant. The correct collocation to use in legal English is "to serve (the document) on someone".

Associated Words: Served (past simple), Served (3rd form), Service (noun), To Serve (documents) on someone (collocation), Claim (noun), Claimant (noun), Claim Form (noun), Defendant (noun), To Issue (verb).

Solicitor (person): A solicitor is a qualified legal advisor who has finished their law studies and practical training to become a lawyer in England and Wales. However, in England and Wales there are two types of lawyer (see barrister above). A solicitor gives legal advice, researches legal points, drafts letters and contracts and represents clients in court. The main difference between a barrister and a solicitor is that a solicitor needs a higher "right of audience" to represent clients in the higher courts, for example, the Court of Appeal. A right of audience is permission to represent and speak for your client in court. Barristers automatically have higher rights of audience.

Associated Words: Advocacy (noun), Barrister (person), Court (noun), Court of Appeal (noun).

Statement of Case (noun): This is a formal document used in civil litigation in which a party can state their arguments or positions. For example, the particulars of claim, the defence and the reply to defence are all statements of case. There are rules in the Civil Procedure Rules that provide for the form and the time limits when all statements of case must be filed with the court and served on other parties.

Associated Words: Case (noun), Claim (noun), Civil Procedure Rules (noun), To File a Document (collocation), To Serve a Document (collocation).

Statement of Truth (noun): This is a phrase that follows certain documents stating that the contents of the documents are true. In civil litigation all statements of case, witness statements, acknowledgements of service and many other types of documents have a statement of truth. For example, a witness statement must include the phrase "I believe that the facts as stated in the witness statement are true". The witness must then sign the statement of truth.

Associated Words: Acknowledgement of Service (noun), Case (noun), Witness Statement (noun).

To Submit (verb): This means to suggest or propose. It is used in legal English when an advocate suggests or states an opinion to the court. For example, "I submit to the court that Mrs Jones breached her duty of care to the claimant". At the end of the trial both advocates give "submissions" to the court. This is similar to a summary of the evidence of their case.

Associated Words: Submitted (past simple), Submitted (3rd form), Submission (noun), To Breach (verb), Case (noun), Claimant (noun), Duty of Care (noun), Loss (noun), Trial (noun).

Third Party (noun): This is a party who may not be a part of the proceedings, but they do have an interest or receive a type of benefit or detriment in relation to the claim.

Associated Words: Claim (noun), Party (noun), Proceedings (noun).

3 DEFENDING A CLAIM

Acknowledgement of Service (noun): This is a document that the defendant must complete and file at court. The document asks the defendant if they admit, deny or acknowledge the claim. To acknowledge means that you know something has happened or that it exists.
Associated Words: To Acknowledge (verb), To Admit (verb), Defendant (noun), To Deny (verb).

To Admit (verb): To admit something means that you confess that you did it or that you are liable for something you did.
Associated Words: Admitted (past simple), Admitted (3rd Form), Admission (noun), Liable (adjective).

Contributory Negligence (noun): This means that the defendant alleges that the claimant caused some of the harm or loss suffered in the claim. If the court agree, then the amount of damages awarded to the claimant may be reduced. This is because the court believes that the claimant contributed to their own loss.
Associated Words: To Allege (verb), To Cause (verb), Claim (noun), Claimant (noun), Harm (noun), Loss (noun).

To Counterclaim (verb): A counterclaim is a claim made by the defendant against the claimant regarding the same or related issues as the claimant's original claim.
Associated Words: Counterclaimed (past simple), Counterclaimed (3rd

form), Counterclaim (noun), Claimant (noun), Defendant (noun).

Default Judgment (noun): This is a ruling by the court that means that one party wins the case because of a failure to act or a lack of response from the other party. It is common for a claimant to be granted default judgment (also known as judgment in default) when a defendant does not respond to a claim.

Associated Words: Claim (noun), Claimant (noun), Defendant (noun), To Be Granted Judgment in Default (collocation).

To Defend (verb): This verb means that you deny all or some of the allegations stated in the claim form and particulars of claim. The statement of case for a defendant is called a defence and must be filed at court and served on the other parties. The defence will explain the defendant's version of the events that are stated by the claimant in the particulars of claim and the claim form.

Associated Words: Defended (past simple), Defended (3rd form), Defence (noun), Defendant (noun), Allegation (noun), Claim (noun), Claimant (noun), To Deny (verb), To File at Court (collocation), Particulars of Claim (noun), To Serve on a Party (collocation), Statement of Case (noun).

To Deny (verb): To deny something means to state that you did not do something or that you are not liable for something. It is opposite to the verb to admit. The collocation "to deny allegations" is very common in civil litigation and dispute resolution.

Associated Words: Denied (past simple), Denied (3rd form), Denial (noun), Denied (adjective), Denial (noun), To Admit (verb), Allegations (noun), Liable (adjective).

Mitigation of Loss (collocation): This is a concept in common law that means that a person who has suffered loss must take reasonable action to stop or reduce any further loss or damage. If the defendant can establish in court that the claimant did not mitigate their loss, the court may reduce the award for damages to the claimant.

Associated Words: To Mitigate (verb), To Award (verb), Claimant (noun), Common Law (noun), Damages (noun), Loss (noun), To Suffer (verb).

To Respond (verb): The verb to respond means to answer or reply. For instance, under the provisions of the Civil Procedure Rules, once a defendant receives a claim form they have a set period of time in which to respond.

Associated Words: Responded (past simple), Responded (3rd form), Response (noun), Claim Form, (noun), Civil Procedure Rules (noun).

4 COURT PROCEEDINGS

Admissible (adjective): Admissible evidence is evidence that is allowed or admitted to court. Most evidence is admissible, but an example of inadmissible evidence is hearsay evidence. Hearsay evidence is evidence that is told to the witness and not actually seen or heard by the witness themselves. This is not usually admissible in court.

Associated Words: To Admit (verb), Hearsay (noun), Witness (person).

To Allocate (verb): To allocate means to assign or designate and is used in legal English when the court chooses the correct track for a claim to proceed on. In civil litigation there are three choices: small claims court, fast track and multi-track. The court will look at the characteristics of the claim including the amount of damages claimed, the complexity of the issues and the importance of the claim. The parties must complete a document called the 'Directions Questionnaire'. The court will then allocate the claim to a track. Usually, if a claim is complicated or of a large monetary value, the court will allocate the claim to the multi-track. Each track has its own rules for how the claim proceeds.

Associated Words: Allocated (past simple), Allocated (3ʳᵈ form), Allocation (noun), Claim (noun), Damages (noun), Directions Questionnaire (noun), Small Claims Court (noun), Fast Track (noun), Multi-Track (noun).

Application (noun): In legal English an application is a request for something from the court or other party. The collocation used is "to make an application". For example, an application can be made to the court for further disclosure from another party. Sometimes the court will want to schedule a hearing to hear the arguments in order to make a ruling on the application. The word 'application' is also the name for the document or court form used. There are many different types of application and the correct form must be used to make the right application to the court. There are many rules in the Civil Procedure Rules in relation to time limits and procedure for applications.

Associated Words: To Make an Application (collocation), Civil Procedure Rules (noun), Disclosure (noun), To Hear (verb).

Case Management Conference "CMC" (noun): A case management conference is a hearing in which the issues, timetable and procedure of the claim is organised. For instance, a case management conference can give directions on disclosure of documents, witness statements, expert reports, etc. The CMCs are seen as a very important part of the process, especially with multi-track claims. It is common for the court to schedule a CMC soon after the particulars of claim and defence have been filed in order for the issues to be identified quickly.

Associated Words: Claim (noun), Defence (noun), Disclosure (noun), Expert (person), To File (verb), Hearing (noun), Issues (noun), Multi-Track (noun), Particulars of Claim (noun), Witness Statement (noun).

Conditional Fee Agreement (noun): This is an agreement between a lawyer and their client where it is agreed that a fee is only payable for the lawyer's services if the case results in a favourable conclusion for the client. This means that the lawyer is only paid if the client wins the case or if the claim is settled out of court. The fee is then taken as a percentage of the money won or received in settlement. These agreements are also known as "No-win no-fee" agreements. If the case is lost, the lawyer is not paid for their services.

Associated Words: Case (noun), Claim (noun), To Settle (verb).

Counsel (person): Counsel is an alternative word usually used for a barrister, however, it can also be used for an advocate and so the phrase "counsel for the claimant" means the lawyer representing the claimant.

Associated Words: Barrister (person), Claimant (noun).

Directions (noun): These are orders from the court that must be complied with by the parties. They are usually procedural obligations that the court feel are necessary for the smooth running of the proceedings. Directions can be agreed by the parties by using a consent order, or the parties may have to attend court for a hearing or case management conference for the directions to be ordered by the court. A common collocation is "the court gives the following directions:"

Associated Words: To Direct (verb), To Give Directions (collocation), Case Management Conference (noun), Comply With (phrasal verb), Consent Order (noun), Hearing (noun), Party (noun), Proceedings (noun).

Directions Questionnaire (noun): This is an official court document that must be completed by the parties to assist the court to decide which track the claim should proceed on.

Associated Words: Claim (noun), Party (noun).

Disclosure (noun): This is the process of stating what documents a party knows exist and are relevant to the claim. This includes stating all the documents which you wish to rely on and, very importantly, all documents that exist but do not help your claim. It is fundamental to the Civil Procedure Rules that each party provides full disclosure of all relevant documents both with documents that assist their case and those that do not. If a party states that a document exists, the other parties may then inspect this document and vice versa. Some documents may exist but do not have to be shown to the court or to other parties. These include documents that are privileged, documents that are marked "without prejudice" or documents that may damage the public interest. The schedule for the full disclosure of documents is usually set out in the case management conference, but disclosure is an ongoing obligation throughout proceedings.

Associated Words: Claim (noun), Case Management Conference (noun), Civil Procedure Rules (noun), Privilege (noun), Without Prejudice (noun).

Fast Track (noun): This is the system used in the Civil Procedure Rules that generally deals with claims that are worth less than £25,000. The concept of the fast track is to deal with these lower value, yet substantial, cases effectively in accordance with the overriding objective. For example, under the fast track the court will try to schedule a final hearing within 30 weeks from the date the case was allocated.

Associated Words: To Allocate (verb), Case (noun), Claim (noun), Civil Procedure Rules (noun), Hearing (noun), Overriding Objective (noun).

To Hear (verb): In legal English this verb means listening to the advocates in court. For example, "the case will be heard next Monday at 12pm". The noun "hearing" is also very common in legal English. It is used when the advocates and judge(s) meet in court to discuss the case. For example, "the hearing is scheduled for 12th March".

Associated Words: Heard (past simple), Heard (3rd form), Hearing (noun), Advocate (person), Court (noun), Judge (person).

Instructions to Counsel (noun): This is a document drafted by a solicitor to a barrister. It is a request for advice or assistance in relation to a specific question of law or in request for representation of the solicitor's client in court.

Associated Words: To Advise (verb), Barrister (person), To Represent (verb), Solicitor (person).

Jurisdiction (noun): This word is used when a court has the authority or the right to hear and decide cases in that area of law and in that location. In legal English lawyers say that the court "has jurisdiction" to hear the case. For example, the Supreme Court has jurisdiction to hear appeal cases sent from the Court of Appeal in England and Wales. This means that they have the authority or the right to hear these cases.

Associated Words: To have Jurisdiction (collocation), Court (noun), To Hear (verb), Right (noun).

Legal Professional Privilege (noun): This is a right that belongs to a lawyer's client which ensures that communication (letters, etc) that a client has with their lawyer will stay secret and confidential. Usually in litigation proceedings both parties must allow the other party to see all the relevant documents and evidence in the case. However, communication between a client and their lawyer does not have to be given to the other party because it is privileged and so stays confidential. This privilege belongs to the client, not the lawyer and only the client can choose for a privileged document to

Michael Howard

be shown to the other party. This is called "waiving privilege".
Associated Words: Court (noun), Party (noun), To Waive (verb).

Master (person): This is an official of the High Court of Justice. A Master will sit and hear applications and case management conferences to help organise and schedule timetables for proceedings. It is similar to the role of a judge but they usually deal with procedural matters.
Associated Words: Applications (noun), Case Management Case (noun), To Hear (verb), Judge (person), Matters (noun), Proceedings (noun), To Sit (verb).

Mediation (noun): This is a popular form of alternative dispute resolution. It is a separate process from litigation and its aim is to settle disputes between parties without the need for further litigation.
Associated Words: Dispute (noun), Parties (noun), To Settle (verb).

Multi-Track (noun): This is the system used in the Civil Procedure Rules for claims worth over £25,000 or for claims that have a high level of complexity or importance. A new multi-track claim will usually have a case management conference to schedule all the necessary steps that all parties must take up to the final hearing.
Associated Words: Case Management Conference (noun), Claim (noun), Civil Procedure Rules (noun), Hearing (noun), Parties (noun).

Part 36 Offer (noun): Part 36 of the Civil Procedure Rules deals with offers to settle. A party can make an offer to settle with or without using Part 36, however, if they choose to use Part 36 then it could help them later if the claim goes to a final hearing. Part 36 offers are confidential between the parties. The court will not know they exist until after judgment has been given. The reason for this is that Part 36 is trying to help the parties settle the case. The concept is, that if a defendant makes a reasonable offer to the claimant before the trial, then the claimant should accept this offer. This is important because if the claimant does not accept a reasonable offer, they will be punished for this when the court decides what percentage of costs the defendant must pay to the claimant. Let's look at an example: During legal proceedings the defendant makes a confidential Part 36 offer to the claimant of £30,000. The claimant rejects the offer and the case continues

23

and goes to trial. At the trial, the judge (who does not know about the Part 36 offer) decides that the defendant is liable and should pay the claimant £20,000. The claimant wins the case, but the amount awarded by the court is less than the defendant's Part 36 offer. The concept here is that the claimant should have accepted the Part 36 offer and should not have continued the claim. The court may then order that the claimant acted unreasonably when they rejected the Part 36 offer and so have to pay their own costs.

Associated Words: Claim (noun), Claimant (noun), Costs (noun), Defendant (noun), Hearing (noun), Liable (adjective), To Offer to Settle (collocation), To Order (verb), To Settle (verb).

Recorder (person): This is an official of the judiciary. They sit as part-time judges in both civil and criminal law systems. There are also Honorary Recorders who are senior judges of certain jurisdictions.

Associated Words: Judge (person), Judiciary (noun), Jurisdiction (noun), To Sit (verb).

Reply to Defence (noun): This is a statement of case that gives the claimant a chance to provide a written response to the defendant's arguments stated in the defence.

Associated Words: Claimant (noun), Defendant (noun), Statement of Case (noun).

Small Claims Court (noun): This is the system that deals with low value proceedings. Usually, if a claimant is claiming less than £10,000 the claim will be allocated to the small claims court. The limit is only a guideline and some cases at higher value will also be allocated to the small claims court if their claim is seen as very simple. The advantage of the small claims court is that there are less procedural obligations for the parties and the claim is dealt with very quickly.

Associated Words: To Allocate (verb), Case (noun), Claim (noun), Claimant (noun), Obligations (noun), Parties (noun).

Stay of Proceedings (noun): This is an order from the court that the proceedings are stopped for a period of time. It is common for claims to be stayed for a certain length of time, but it is also possible for proceedings to be stayed indefinitely. Indefinitely means that there is no specific time limit. Stays are also sometimes known as 'Tomlin Orders', named after the judge who introduced the concept to the courts.

Associated Words: Claim (noun), Order (noun), Proceedings (noun).

Standstill Agreement (noun): This is an agreement when the parties agree to "stop time" so that the limitation period is extended. It is common when certain other investigations or proceedings must conclude before a claim can continue in the courts.

Associated Words: Claim (noun), Limitation Period (noun).

Summary Judgment (noun): This is a judgment from the court that orders that the claimant's case has no real prospect of success or that the defendant has no real prospect of successfully defending the claim. The court will then find in favour of the other party.

Associated Words: Case (noun), Claim (noun), Claimant (noun), To Defend (verb), Defendant (noun), To Find in Favour (collocation), Judgment (noun), To Order (verb), Party (noun).

5 TRIAL

Balance of Probabilities (noun): This is the standard of proof that the claimant must satisfy to be successful in their claim. This means that in civil litigation a claimant must prove their claim is more likely to have happened than not. It is a completely different standard of proof from criminal law, where the standard of proof is to be sure of the guilt of the defendant. This was previously known as beyond reasonable doubt.

Associated Words: Case (noun), Claim (noun), Claimant (noun), Defendant (noun), Standard of Proof (noun).

To Bind (verb): This means that a law, common or statute, must be obeyed and followed by the court. It is used in common law where, for example, a court of first instance must follow the decisions of higher courts. This is called the doctrine of precedent. Rulings or judgments of the higher courts create precedents. These precedents "bind" the lower courts. This means that the lower courts must follow the principles of law set by the higher courts. In legal English it is said that the precedent is "binding", meaning it must be followed.

Associated Words: Bound (past simple), Bound (3rd form), Binding (adjective), To be Bound by Precedent/the Court (collocation), Common Law (noun), Judgment (noun), Precedent (noun).

Closing Statement/Submissions (noun): This is the final part of the advocacy in the trial. Each advocate, for all of the parties in the claim, will give a closing statement to the court. This is also known as making submissions. The advocate will summarise their arguments in an attempt to convince the court to rule in their favour.

Associated Words: Advocate (person), To Give a Closing Statement (collocation), To Make Submissions (collocation), To Rule (verb), To summarise (verb), Trial (noun).

Consent Order (noun): This is an order from the court that has been agreed in advance by all the parties. Usually, a consent order will agree the procedural aspects of the case that are not in dispute.

Associated Words: Case (noun), Dispute (noun), Order (noun), Parties (noun).

Contempt of Court (noun): If a person or organisation does not comply with or obey the rules and orders of the court, then they will be held in contempt of court. It is usually used in relation to the parties' behaviour in court but also it is used to ensure that any media reporting of cases is complicit with the rules and regulations of the court.

Associated Words: To be Held in Contempt of Court (collocation), To Comply With (phrasal verb), To Obey (verb), Order (noun), Party (noun).

Cross-Examination (noun): This means that an advocate asks questions to a witness from another party in the claim. For example, Mr Robinson sues Mr Dibbs. In court Mr Robinson's advocate (a barrister or a solicitor) will first ask Mr Robinson questions about his claim. This is called examination-in-chief. After these questions, Mr Dibbs' advocate will ask Mr Robinson questions about his claim. This is called cross-examination. Later, Mr Robinson's advocate will get a chance to cross-examine Mr Dibbs and his witnesses.

Associated Words: Advocate (person), Barrister (noun), Claim (noun), Party (noun), Solicitor (noun), To Sue (verb).

To Examine (verb): This means to ask questions in court. There are three main types: examination-in-chief, cross-examination and re-examination.

Associated Words: Examined (past simple), Examined (3rd form), Cross-examination (noun), Examination (noun).

Examination-in-Chief (noun): This is the process of an advocate asking questions to their client and their witnesses in court. After a witness is examined by their own advocate, the witness is then cross-examined by opposing advocates.
Associated Words: Advocate (person), Cross-examine (verb), Witness (person).

Expert Witness (person): This is a person who the court believes can assist proceedings because of their specialist knowledge on a particular subject. For instance, psychologists, accountants and childcare workers are examples of expert witnesses.
Associated Words: Party (noun), Proceedings (noun).

To Give Judgment (collocation): This means that the judge(s) have made a decision and are ready to give their reasons for the decision. These reasons for the decision come in the form of a judgment. The collocation to give judgment means that the judge reads the reasoning behind the decision to the parties in court.
Associated Words: Gave judgment (past simple), Given Judgment (3rd form), Judge (person).

To Grant (verb): In legal English this means that something is given or allowed to happen. For instance, if a party requests the chance to appeal a judgment, the court may agree and so will 'grant' leave to appeal. This means that it gives the party permission to appeal the judgment.
Associated Words: Granted (past simple), Granted (3rd form), To Appeal (verb), Judgment (noun), Party (noun).

Leave (noun): This word means permission to do something. In legal English it is used when the court permits a party to appeal a judgment or allows an application to be made to appeal.
Associated Words: To Appeal (verb), Application (noun), Judgment (noun), Party (noun).

Liable (adjective): This means that a party is legally responsible for their actions or omissions. Omissions means that a party did not do something that they should have done. If a party is liable then the court will usually order the liable party to remedy the damage or problem. This can be with money, known as damages, or action, known as an injunction.

Associated Words: Damages (noun), Injunction (noun), Party (noun).

Opening Statement (noun): This is the first speech by the advocate in court. An advocate will usually use this opportunity to explain to the court what the basis of his client's argument and position is. Each party will have a chance to give an opening statement to the court. Once this has been completed by all parties, the evidential part of the trial with the examination of witnesses will begin.

Associated Words: Advocate (person), Evidence (noun), To Examine (verb), Party (noun), Witness (person).

Precedent (noun): This meaning of the word precedent is in relation to common law. Historically, judgments of the courts were written down, also known as "recorded". Over the centuries that followed, a system of following the decisions of the higher courts became usual practice. Nowadays the system of following precedent is one of the most important doctrines of the English legal system. The process is fairly simple. The judgments of the higher courts (Supreme Court and Court of Appeal) must be followed by the lower courts (High Court, County Court, etc). For example, if there is a case about a dispute over a point of law, the lawyers will check the records of the Supreme Court and the Court of Appeal to see if there is a ruling from these courts that will tell them what was decided in similar cases before. If the facts and situations of the cases are very similar then the court must follow this precedent. If the facts and situation are not so similar then the court does not have to follow the precedent. Each judgment will have a part called the "ratio decidendi". This is the part of the judgment which forms the precedent and the part that should be followed by the lower courts. This is the doctrine of "binding precedents".

Associated Words: To Bind (verb), Court of Appeal (noun), County Court (noun), High Court (noun), Judgment (noun), Ratio Decidendi (noun), Supreme Court (noun).

Re-examination (noun): This means that an advocate may ask his client and their witnesses more questions after the opposing advocates have completed their cross-examination. The advocate may only ask questions relating to issues that were raised during cross-examination by the opposing advocates.

Associated Words: Advocate (person), Cross-examination (noun), Witness (person).

Reserve Judgment (noun): This means that the judge(s) decide to spend more time considering their decision. The judges will usually tell the parties at the end of the trial that they wish to reserve judgment and will notify the parties when they have reached a verdict. There are no rules for the time limits but the length of time usually depends on the length and complexity of the case.

Associated Words: Judge (person), Parties (noun), Verdict (noun).

To Seek (verb): In normal everyday English, this verb means to look for something, however, in legal English it is used by advocate to ask the court to make an order or to find in their favour. Common collocations are "to seek an order from the court", or " to seek judgment in the (claimant's) favour".

Associated Words: Sought (past simple), Sought (3rd form), Judgment (noun), Order (noun).

Summons (noun): This is a document from the court that orders a person to attend court to give evidence or to produce an exhibit or document.

Associated Words: Evidence (noun), Exhibit (noun), To Order (verb).

Verdict (noun): This means the decision of the judge or court.

Associated Words: Judge (person), To Reach a Verdict (collocation).

Witness (person): This is a person who can assist the court with a claim. A witness can be an actual witness, known as an eye-witness, an expert witness or someone who knows something in relation to the claim and can help the court reach its verdict.

Associated Words: Claim (noun), Expert (person), To Reach a Verdict (collocation).

6 AFTER THE TRIAL

To Appeal (verb): To appeal means to ask a higher court or tribunal to review a decision or judgment to reverse or overrule part or all of it. There are many reasons why a judgment is appealed. For example, it could be appealed because the judge(s) made a mistake with the law or because new evidence has appeared in the case. The process for appealing is simple. Usually, a special application or request is made to the court. In some cases permission (or "leave") of the court must be obtained to allow the application. If the appeal is allowed, the appellate court will hear the case again. The party who applies for the appeal is called the appellant and the other party is called the respondent. A common collocation used in legal English is "appeal against the judgment/verdict/decision")

Associated Words: Appealed (past simple), Appealed (3rd form), Appealed (adjective), Appeal (noun), To Appeal against something (collocation), Appellant (noun), Appellate Court (noun), Court (noun), Evidence (noun), To Hear (verb), Judgment (noun), Party (noun), Respondent (noun).

Appellant (noun): This is a party who appeals against a verdict or decision of a court or tribunal.

Associated Words: To Appeal (verb), To Appeal against something (collocation), Party (noun), Verdict (noun).

Attachment of Earnings Order (noun): This is a ruling from the court that orders the defendant to pay a judgment debt directly from their salary or wages. The court will usually order that a percentage of the defendant's salary will automatically be transferred to the claimant every week or every month.

Associated Words: Debt (noun), Defendant (noun), Judgment Debt (noun), To Order (verb).

To Award (verb): This verb is used when the court grants a remedy to a party in the claim. An example of a common collocation is "the court awarded the claimant £50,000 in damages".

Associated Words: Claim (noun), Claimant (noun), Damages (noun), To Grant (verb), Remedy (noun).

Bailiff (person): This is a person who has authority from the court to collect unpaid judgment debts. The bailiff collects money or property owned by the defendant which can then be sold for the equal amount of the debt.

Associated Words: Debt (noun), Judgment (noun).

Bankruptcy (noun): This word is very common in the English legal system and describes the situation when the court declares that an individual, sole trader or partnership does not have enough money to pay its debts. This term is commonly misunderstood with the term insolvency. If you do not have enough money to pay all your debts, you are insolvent. You are not bankrupt until the court officially declares that you are unable to pay all your debts. Also, the term bankruptcy is used in England and Wales only in relation to individuals, sole traders and partnerships. The term is not used in relation to companies in England and Wales.

Associated Words: Bankrupt (adjective), To Go Bankrupt (collocation), To Be Declared Bankrupt by the Court (collocation).

Charge (noun): This is a legal right that one party has over the property or assets of another party. It is used when one party does not have enough money to pay a judgment debt. For example, the court finds in favour of the claimant and awards the claimant £50,000 in damages. The defendant submits that they do not have £50,000, but they do own a house. The court can order that a charge is put on the defendant's property to the value of £50,000 in favour of the claimant. This means that when the defendant sells the house, the claimant will be paid £50,000 from the money of the sale.

The money from the sale of a house is called the proceeds of sale.

Associated Words: Claimant (noun), Debt (noun), Defendant (noun), In Favour Of (collocation), Judgment (noun), Order (noun).

To Comply With (phrasal verb): This means to obey or follow a request. It is used in relation to judgments and orders. A party must comply with a court order, for example to pay damages to the other party or to comply with an injunction.

Associated Words: Damages (noun), Injunction (noun), Judgment (noun), Order (noun), Party (noun).

Compound Interest (noun): This is money that must be paid in addition to judgment debt interest. Usually, if the claimant is successful, damages are awarded plus interest. Interest is calculated as a percentage of the damages. If the defendant does not pay the damages to the defendant on time, the interest rate increases to a higher rate. This higher rate of interest is called compound interest. It is used as financial punishment for the late or non-payment of a judgment debt. For example, the court finds Mr Green liable and awards Mrs Brown £15,000 in damages plus interest at 6%. If Mr Green does not pay the damages to Mrs Brown on time, then the interest rate will increase to 10% for the amount that is paid late. The interest charged at 10% is the compound interest. It is only applied to the payments Mr Green does not pay on time to Mrs Brown.

Associated Words: To Award (verb), Claimant (noun), Damages (noun), Debt (noun), Defendant (noun), Interest (noun), Judgment (noun).

Consequential Loss (noun): This is indirect loss suffered by the defendant. For instance, Miss Anderson causes a bad car accident in which Miss Wright was badly injured. Miss Wright may claim damages for the "direct" loss suffered such as medical bills and repairs to her car. However, she may also claim for "indirect loss" such as loss of salary if she has to take time off work. The loss of salary is a "consequence" of the accident and so this type of loss is called consequential loss. The concept arose from common law in England and Wales.

Associated Words: To Claim (verb), Common Law (noun), Damages (noun), Loss (noun), To Suffer (verb).

Costs (noun): This means the cost of bringing and hearing legal proceedings. In legal English it usually means the fees of the court, barristers, solicitors and the experts who charge for their services. It is a very important concept in legal English as the usual rule is that the party who is unsuccessful must pay the costs of the successful party. In many smaller cases the costs are easily dealt with by the court. This is called a summary assessment. However, in more complicated claims there will be a separate hearing on the issue of costs and an independent expert is appointed to calculate the costs of the parties. This is called a detailed assessment. The Civil Procedure Rules provides guidelines on the rules of costs in proceedings, but it is a very complicated and constantly changing area of law.

Associated Words: Barrister (person), Civil Procedure Rules (noun), Detailed Assessment (noun), Expert (person), Proceedings (noun), Solicitor (person).

Costs on an Indemnity Basis (collocation): This means that the court orders the losing party to pay a high percentage of the winning party's costs.

Associated Words: Case (noun), Costs (noun), Party (noun), Verdict (noun).

Costs on a Standard Basis (collocation): This means the court orders the losing party to pay a reasonable percentage of the winning party's costs.

Associated Words: Case (noun), Costs (noun), Party (noun), Verdict (noun).

Damages (noun): This is the legal English word for compensation or money paid by the liable party to the successful party. Please note that this noun is already plural and does not have a singular form. The noun "damage" means broken and is not a legal English term. Accordingly, the two words, damage and damages are completely different and should not be confused. Damages is a very important concept of civil litigation and this is the most common remedy awarded by the courts.

Associated Words: Liable (noun), Party (noun), Remedy (noun).

Declaration (noun): This is a judgment or award from the court that states a party's rights or legal relationships with other parties. This type of

judgment is commonly known as a declaratory judgment.
Associated Words: Award (noun), Judgment (noun).

Detailed Assessment (noun): This is a special procedure where a court will investigate the costs of proceedings to determine whether they are proportionate to the case and how much the unsuccessful party must pay to the successful party.
Associated Words: Costs (noun), Party (noun).

To Enforce (verb): This verb means to make sure that a person or organisation does what they have been ordered to do. The best example of a common collocation in legal English is that a judgment is enforced. This means that the court has authority to force or make sure that the judgment is effective and that all court orders have been complied with. For example, Mr Ball issues a claim against Mrs Clark for £10,000. Mr Ball wins his claim and so the court orders that Mrs Clark must pay £10,000 (plus interest) to Mr Ball in damages. The court gives Mrs Clark 60 days to pay the sum in full. If she does not pay within 60 days, Mr Ball can enforce the judgment. This means he has the right to ask the court to force Mrs Clark to pay the money. This can include asking for a legal charge over property or using the services of a bailiff.
Associated Words: Charge (noun), Claim (noun), Judgment (noun), Order (noun).

To Find (verb): In legal English this verb means to decide or conclude. For instance, the court will "find in favour of the claimant" or "find that a witness is not credible".
Associated Words: Found (past simple), Found (3rd form), Case (noun), Claimant (noun), To Find in Favour (collocation), Witness (person).

To Find in Favour (collocation): This collocation means that the judge(s) have reached a decision and that one of the parties has won the case. Judges(s) can find in favour of either party (the claimant or the defendant) and in both of these situations the collocation to find in favour can be used.
Associated Words: Found in Favour (past simple), Found in Favour (3rd form), Case (noun), Claimant (noun), Defendant (noun), Judge (person), Party (noun).

Freezing Order (noun): This is an order of the court that stops a party to the proceedings from transferring their assets, usually money in a bank account, out of the jurisdiction of the court. It is usually ordered to stop potential problems in relation to the payment of the judgment debts. It is also known as Mareva Order or a Mareva Injunction.

Associated Words: Debt (noun), Injunction (noun), Judgment (noun), Jurisdiction (noun), Order (noun), Party (noun), Proceedings (noun).

Injunction (noun): This is a type of remedy available from the court. An injunction is an order from the court that states that a party must do something, or stop from doing something. A party who does not follow or obey an injunction can be liable in both criminal and civil law and can face serious penalties if they do not comply with the injunction.

Associated Words: To Comply With (collocation), Order (noun), Party (noun), Remedy (noun).

Interest (noun): This means extra money that can be claimed in addition to damages. It is usually a percentage of the amount of damages claimed.

Associated Word: Damages (noun).

Joint and Several Liability (collocation): This phrase means that if there is a group of two or more people who are liable for a judgment debt, then all of the members of the group are liable individually and also together as a group. For example, if Mr and Mrs Benson are liable for damages, the court may order that the liability is joint and several. This means that Mr Smith is liable for all of the debt, Mrs Smith is liable for all the debt, and together Mr and Mrs Smith are liable for the debt. The court can enforce the judgment against both Mr and Mrs Benson individually or together.

Associated Words: Damages (noun), To Enforce (verb), Liable (noun), To Order (verb).

Judgment Debt (noun): A debt is money owed by one person or organisation to another. A judgment debt is money that must be paid by a party to another party by order of the court.

Associated Words: Debt (noun), Judgment (noun), Order (noun), Party (noun).

Loss (noun): This means the reduction in value of something that has been damaged, broken or injured. It is a very important concept in civil litigation and dispute resolution as loss must be suffered for compensation to be paid. It is the basis of claims in both tort and contract law and must be established before the court for a claim to be successful.

Associated Words: Claim (noun), Contract Law (noun), Dispute Resolution (noun), Litigation (noun), To Suffer (verb).

Obligation (noun): An obligation is something that a person must do. An obligation can be legal or moral but within the English legal system it is common to see the words "duties and obligations" especially in commercial contracts. This means that the parties to the contract must do (or must not do) whatever is written in this section of the contract. In legal English the phrase "to fulfil an obligation" is very common. To fulfil an obligation means to complete it.

Associated Words: Contract Law (noun), To Fulfil an Obligation (collocation), Party (noun).

To Order (verb): This means that the court states that something must be done, stopped or prohibited from being done. The noun "order" is the document used to state the orders of the court. The collocation used is "to make an order".

Associated Words: Ordered (past simple), Ordered (3rd form), Order (noun), To Make an Order (collocation).

Remedy (noun): This word is used to describe the way a court will try to compensate or resolve the harm or loss that the claimant has suffered. There are three main types of remedy in civil litigation. The most common is damages. This is monetary compensation awarded to the claimant to compensate them for their loss. The second, called equitable remedies, are injunctions and specific performance. These are court orders that specify that a particular action must be taken or is prohibited. The third are declaratory judgments which state the rights or legal relationships between parties.

Associated Words: To Remedy (verb), Claimant (noun), Damages (noun), Declaratory Judgment (noun), Equitable (noun), Harm (noun), Injunction (noun), Loss (noun), To Order (verb), Specific Performance (noun).

Remoteness (noun): Remoteness is a concept in relation to damages. Common law states that damages can only be awarded to an injured party where the loss was not too remote. This means that the loss suffered must be within the reasonable contemplation of the parties. This means that the loss suffered must be reasonably predictable at the time of the breach. The rule is used to stop claims where claimants are unreasonable in the amount and the reasons for their claim.

Associated Words: To Award (verb), Claim (noun), Claimant (noun), Common Law (noun), Damages (noun), Injured Party (noun), Party (noun), To Suffer (verb).

To Rescind (verb): This verb is used as a remedy to cancel a contract between parties. The principle of the remedy is to put all the parties back in the position they were in before they entered into the contract. In England and Wales, the court has the power to rescind a contract in certain situations.

Associated Words: Party (noun), Remedy (noun).

Respondent (noun): This is a party who is served an appeal notice by an appellant and, accordingly, must respond to the notice.

Associated Words: To Appeal (verb), Party (noun).

Restitution (noun): This is a type of remedy from the court. Usually the court will order compensation to be paid by the defendant for the loss suffered by the claimant in the form of damages. However, in some situations the loss suffered by the claimant may be very small. The court has the option to order restitution. The law of restitution means that the court orders the defendant to pay their profits that resulted from their breach of contract to the claimant. For example, Mr Burgess issues proceedings against Mr Shaw for breach of contract. Mr Burgess did not actually suffer any loss as a result of Mr Shaw's breach, but if Mr Shaw profited greatly from the result of his breach, then the court can order restitution and order that Mr Shaw pay his profits from his breach of contract to Mr Burgess.

Associated Words: To Breach (verb), Claimant (noun), Damages (noun), Defendant (noun), Loss (noun), To Order (verb), Remedy (noun), To Suffer (verb).

Search Order (noun): This is a court order that states that a property can be searched and evidence seized without warning. Seized means that the property is taken and held in a safe place by the authorities. Clearly, this order is only used in the most exceptional and serious situations. For example, the court will order a search order (or warrant) when the court believes there is a danger that evidence will be destroyed by the defendant. This order was previously known as an Anton Piller order as it was named after a case of the same name.
Associated Words: Evidence (noun), Order (noun).

Specific Performance (noun): This is a remedy from the court that orders a party to do a certain act. Usually specific performance is ordered to make a party fulfil their obligations under a contract. It is an alternative remedy when damages are perhaps not relevant to the claim as the claimant has not actually suffered any loss.
Associated Words: Claim (noun), Claimant (noun), Damages (noun), To Fulfil an Obligation (collocation), Loss (noun), To Order (verb), Remedy (noun), To Suffer (verb).

Summary Assessment (noun): This is a special procedure when the court will deal with the costs of the case fairly quickly and without the need for costs proceedings or detailed assessment of costs. Summary assessment is common for lower value, simple claims.
Associated Words: Claim (noun), Costs (noun), Detailed Assessment (noun).

Vexatious Litigation (noun): This means that a claimant issues a number of claims that are totally without merit. Without merit means that there are no grounds or good reasons to make the claim. Vexatious litigants are usually placed on a special list and must ask the court for permission to issue a claim with the court. The courts are generally reluctant to place a litigant on the list as it restricts their access to the courts. It is, therefore, not common for litigants to be placed on the list without good reason.
Associated Words: Claim (noun), Claimant (noun), Grounds (noun), To Issue a Claim (collocation).

Warrant of Execution (noun): This is a court document that grants permission to a bailiff to collect a judgment debt. This may include entering a debtor's property and taking their possessions. These possessions are then sold to collect money to pay the judgment debt.

Associated Words: Bailiff (person), Debt (noun), To Grant (verb), Judgment Debt (noun)

7 TYPES OF PROCEEDINGS AND CLAIMS

Breach of Contract (noun): The verb "to breach" is the legal term that means to break. If there is a breach of contract it means that one party to the contract has not fulfilled their obligations under that contract. In other words, they have "broken" the contract. As a result of this, the injured party may bring proceedings for breach of contract. These types of claims are very common in civil litigation and dispute resolution and cover many different areas of law.

Associated Words: Claim (noun), Dispute (noun), To Fulfill an Obligation (collocation), Injured Party (noun), Proceedings (noun).

Copyright/Trademark/Patent Infringement (noun): This means that a piece of work (book, music, film, etc) has been used without the permission of the owner of the work. Copyright infringement can include copying, publishing, re-producing or re-selling. Other more informal terms for copyright infringement are "piracy" and "copyright theft".

Associated Words: To Infringe (verb).

Defamation (noun): This is the name of the area of law that deals with false, negative statements. Defamation is the communication of a statement made by somebody about somebody else which causes this person to have a negative or worse image or reputation. Defamation can be divided into two areas; slander and libel.

Associated Words: Slander (noun), Libel (noun).

Discrimination (noun): These are proceedings brought by an individual or organisation that means that they believe that they have been treated in a worse way than other people. Common claims for discrimination include racial, gender, religious, age, sexual orientation and disability.
Associated Words: Claim (noun), Proceedings (noun).

Divorce (noun): This means that a married couple do not wish to continue living their lives together in a legal relationship. A divorce is a legal agreement to end the marriage and decides future arrangements in relation to children, property, money and other assets that the couple own. In legal English a married couple "get a divorce" or "get divorced". This agreement must be accepted and approved by the court.
Associated Words: To Divorce (verb), To Get a Divorce (collocation), To Get Divorced (collocation), Court (noun).

Group Litigation (noun): Group litigation is the name for proceedings which have many parties. In this situation the Civil Procedure Rules allow the court to make a Group Litigation Order ("GLO"). A GLO allows all the claimants to bring the claim together as one main claim. These proceedings are usually on a large scale and so involve case management conferences to organise and schedule the obligations of the parties. A lead solicitor is usually appointed to run and manage the GLO.
Associated Words: Claim (noun), Claimant (noun), Civil Procedure Rules (noun), Party (noun), Proceedings (noun).

Harassment (noun): This means that one person or a group of people are acting in an unpleasant, threatening or disturbing way. To threaten means to force someone to do something that they do not want to do and if they do not do it then they will be punished. In civil litigation and dispute resolution, harassment usually happens in two main areas. The first area is at work and is covered by employment law, the second is sexual harassment which is also a criminal offence. An important thing to note in legal English is that in some countries the term "mobbing" is used to describe harassment. Please be careful if you wish to use this term as it is not common in legal English in this context.
Associated Words: Dispute Resolution (noun).

Human Rights (noun): Due to the European Convention on Human Rights and the Human Rights Act 1998, these claims have become increasingly popular in in the English courts. Common claims are brought regarding freedom of speech, right to a fair trial, freedom of religion and freedom of movement and establishment.
Associated Word: Claim (noun).

Insolvency Proceedings (noun): These proceedings are for situations when a company, organisation or individual cannot pay all of their debts. There are a number of options available depending on the specific circumstances of the case, however, commonly the phrase "winding up" is used in legal English to describe the process for companies.
Associated Words: Case (noun), Debt (noun).

Libel (noun): This is a type of defamation. Libel is the written or broadcast communication of a false statement that makes a person or organisation's reputation or image worsen.
Associated Word: Defamation (noun).

Misrepresentation (noun): This is a claim that means that one party persuaded another party to enter into a contract by making false statements about the contract. For instance, Mr Craig wants to buy Mrs Robinson's car. Mrs Robinson tells Mr Craig that her car is 5 years old and has travelled 50,000 kilometers. Mr Craig buys the car but it stops working after one month. Later Mr Craig discovers that the car is actually 10 years old and has travelled 100,000 kilometers. Due to these false statements, Mr Craig can bring a claim against Mrs Robinson for misrepresentation.
Associated Words: To Bring a Claim (collocation).

Negligence (noun): This is a very common type of legal proceeding and means that a party has failed to act in the same way that a reasonable person would do and that this failure caused another person harm or loss. It is similar to the non-legal term "carelessness". It is a large and complex area of law which is governed mostly by common law, although there is some statutory legislation on the subject. To establish negligence a claimant must first show that the defendant owed them a duty of care, second that the defendant breached that duty of care and, third that the breach resulted in

45

the claimant suffering loss. If the claimant can prove all three aspects, then the defendant may be held liable by the court and ordered to pay damages to the claimant. An interesting principle from negligence is that there does not need to be any prior relationship or contract between the parties for a duty of care to be established.

Associated Words: Negligent (adjective), To Breach (verb), Claimant (noun), Damages (noun), Defendant (noun), Duty of Care (noun), Harm (noun), Loss (noun), To Suffer (verb).

Nuisance (noun): This is a common law tort that affects a person's quiet enjoyment of their property. A claim for nuisance can be brought for an action that disturbs or annoys another person, such as loud noise, pollution, dangerous chemicals, etc. The common law remedy for nuisance is damages, but under the law of equity, injunctions are also available from the court.

Associated Words: Claim (noun), Damages (noun), Equity (noun), Injunction (noun), Remedy (noun), Tort (noun).

Personal Injury (noun): This area of law deals with physical suffering. One of the most common negligence claims are for personal injury where a negligent act or omission has caused physical harm. It is a well-established and a large area of civil litigation. Also, the Civil Procedure Rules has a specific pre-action protocol for these types of claims.

Associated Words: To Cause (verb), Claim (noun), Civil Procedure Rules (noun), Harm (noun), Negligence (noun).

Product Liability (noun): This area of law deals with the situation when a person or business buys a defective product. Defective means that the product is broken or is not fit or safe to use. Product liability is an area of law that helps the consumer if they buy something that is not working or does not do what it should. For a product liability claim, a claimant does not need to establish negligence or intention because this tort is a "strict liability" tort.

Associated Words: Harm (noun), Loss (noun), Negligence (noun), Strict Liability (noun), To Suffer (verb), Tort (noun).

Professional Negligence (noun): This is a type of claim in civil litigation. This means that a person who has a special skill or trade is negligent in the way they practice that skill or trade. There is not a specific definition of who is a professional and who is not in legal English. There are specific rules for these types of claims and there is a pre-action protocol in the Civil Procedure Rules which must be followed. These claims are usually brought by clients of specialised workers and such claims can be brought in tort or as a breach of contract.

Associated Words: Breach of Contract (noun), Civil Procedure Rules (noun), Claim (noun), Negligence (noun), To Practice (verb), Tort (noun).

Slander (noun): Slander is one of two types of defamation. Slander generally deals with the spoken communication of a false statement about a person or organisation that creates a worse or negative image or reputation.

Associated Word: Defamation (noun).

Strict Liability (noun): This means that a defendant is legally responsible for damage or loss caused by an act or omission, without the claimant having to prove negligence or intention. Torts such as product liability and some crimes, for instance driving under the influence of alcohol are examples of strict liability.

Associated Words: Claimant (noun), Loss (noun), Negligence (noun), Tort (noun).

Tort Law/The Law of Tort (noun): The law of tort relates to "civil wrongs". It is unique in nature as you do not need to have a contract with someone for the law of tort to operate. In the law of tort there are situations when we owe a duty of care to other people, even to people who we have never met before. In these situations we must be careful not to cause or create any injury or damage in these situations. It is a very complicated and ever-changing area of law and there are thousands of common law cases and precedents that have developed the law of Tort over hundreds of years. Tort law includes negligence (carelessness), nuisance (stopping someone having quiet enjoyment of their home), defamation (slander and libel), false imprisonment and trespass (to land and to the person). It is a common law principle and is designed to compensate the victim. It was not initially designed to punish the person who caused the tort (also known as a "tortfeasor").

Associated Words: Common Law (noun), Defamation (noun), Libel (noun), Negligence (noun), Nuisance (noun), Slander (noun), Precedent (noun).

Trespass (noun): This is a type of tort which can be divided into three parts. The first part is trespass to land which means that somebody is interfering with land or property that they do not own and do not have any rights over. To interfere means that somebody is affecting something in a negative way. For example, if I park my car on my neighbour's garden without permission, I am trespassing. The second type of trespass is trespass to the person. This is unwanted interference with another person. More commonly, trespass to the person is known as battery or assault depending on the act. False imprisonment is also trespass to the person and means that somebody does not allow another person the freedom to move or go where or when they wish to. The third type of trespass is trespass to chattels. Chattels means goods, property or more informally, things. Recently in legal English, trespass to chattels has developed to include claims in respect of spam email and internet server interference.

Associated Words: Claim (noun), Tort (noun).

Unfair Dismissal (noun): This means that an employee's employment contract is terminated without fair grounds or reasons. The employee would bring a claim for unfair dismissal to compensate them for the suffering and loss suffered as a result of the dismissal.

Associated Words: Claim (noun), Grounds (noun), Loss (noun), To Suffer (verb).

Wills and Probate (noun): This is the procedure for distributing the assets and possessions of a person who has died. A will is a document that states the intentions of the person who died. Usually, there is not a dispute in relation to the distribution of a will, however, sometimes the will is contested by the beneficiaries. A beneficiary is a person who receives money or property from the will. If a will is contested, this means that two or more people disagree with the will or the circumstances under which the will was written. Proceedings are then brought to resolve these types of disputes before the courts.

Associated Words: Beneficiary (noun), Dispute (noun), Proceedings (noun), To Resolve (verb).

7 GLOSSARY

Before a Claim

Adjudication
To Allege
Alternative Dispute Resolution
Arbitration
To Breach
Causation
Carelessness
Civil Procedure Rules
To Commit
To Dispute
Duty of Care
Foreseeable
Governing Law
Grounds
To Harm
To Infringe
Injured Party
Letter Before Action
Litigation
Loss
To Omit
Overriding Objective
Practice Direction
Pre-action Protocol
To Resolve
To Settle
To Suffer
Woolf Report

Making a Claim

Affidavit
Barrister
To Brief
To Bring an Action
Burden of Proof
Case
To Claim
Claimant
Claim Form
Court Fee
Evidence
Exhibit
To File
To Issue
Issue
Limitation
Litigant in Person
Particulars of Claim
Plaintiff
To Plead
Proceedings
To Serve
Solicitor
Statement of Case
Statement of Truth
To Submit
Third Party

Defending a Claim

Acknowledgement of service
To Admit
Contributory Negligence
To Counterclaim
Default Judgment
To Defend
To Deny
Mitigation of Loss
To Respond

Court Proceedings

Admissible
To Allocate
Application
Case Management Conference
Conditional Fee Agreement
Counsel
Directions
Directions Questionnaire
Disclosure
Fast Track
To Hear
Instructions to Counsel
Jurisdiction
Legal Professional Privilege
Master
Mediation
Multi-Track
Part 36 Offer
Recorder
Reply to Defence
Small Claims Court
Stay of Proceedings
Standstill Agreement
Summary Judgment

Trial

Balance of Probabilities
To Bind
Closing Statement/Submissions
Consent Order
Contempt of Court
Cross-examination
To Examine
Examination-in-Chief
Expert Witness
To Give Judgment
To Grant
Leave
Liable
Opening statement
Precedent
Re-examination
Reserve Judgment
To Seek
Summons
Verdict
Witness

After the Trial

To Appeal
Appellant
Attachment of Earnings Order
To Award
Bailiff
Bankruptcy
Charge
To Comply With
Compound Interest
Consequential Loss
Costs
Costs on an Indemnity Basis
Costs on a Standard Basis
Damages
Declaration
Detailed Assessment
To Enforce
To Find
To Find in Favour
Freezing Order
Injunction
Interest
Joint and Several Liability
Judgment Debt
Loss
Obligation
To Order
Remedy
Remoteness
To Rescind
Respondent
Restitution
Search Order
Specific Performance

Summary Assessment
Vexatious Litigation
Warrant of Execution

Types of Proceedings and Claims

Breach of Contract
Copyright/Trademark/Patent Infringement
Defamation
Discrimination
Divorce
Group Litigation
Harassment
Human Rights
Insolvency Proceedings
Libel
Misrepresentation
Negligence
Nuisance
Personal Injury
Product Liability
Professional Negligence
Slander
Strict Liability
Tort
Trespass
Unfair Dismissal
Wills and Probate

EXERCISES

8 TRUE OR FALSE

Decide if these sentences are true or false (answers are at the back of the book):

1. To commit is the correct verb to use in legal English when stating that a person has done something criminal or tortious.

2. A dispute is a term lawyers use for an argument or disagreement in legal proceedings.

3. Some types of claims have a pre-action protocol in the Civil Procedure Rules. This is for guidance only and parties do not have to follow it.

4. In a civil claim the claimant has the burden of proof. This means that they must show the court that their version of events is more likely that the defendant's version.

5. If the claim is complicated, legal proceedings can be issued directly at the Supreme Court.

6. The main objective of the Civil Procedure Rules is to ensure a fast, inexpensive and fair legal system in the courts. The rules are not designed for claims to settle before legal proceedings begin.

7. To admit liability means that you state you are not legally responsible for what the claimant has alleged.

8. It is common for defendants to file an acknowledgement of service in

response to a claim form as it gives them more time to reply to the allegations.

9. All parties have to disclose evidence that is relevant to the claim. This includes evidence that does not assist their case or position.

10. A claim in the small claims court will usually have a case management conference. This organises a schedule of obligations for the parties to comply with.

11. In legal English, jurisdiction means that the court has geographical and authoritative power to hear the claim.

12. A consent order is an order from the court that all the parties have agreed for the court to approve.

13. In civil litigation, a judgment from the Court of Appeal can be appealed to the High Court of Justice.

14. A closing statement is made after all the evidence has been heard by the court.

15. A claim can be issued at any time. There is no limitation period that exists for civil claims.

16. On a claim form, the claimant can state the amount they are claiming in damages plus interest.

17. Restitution is when both parties are put back into the position they would have been in if the contract had not existed. It is a common law remedy.

18. If a claim is for less than £10,000 and is a very simple case, then the claim will probably be allocated to the fast track.

19. A person who issues lots of claims for little or no reason is called a vexatious litigant.

20. If there are many claimants and defendants in the same dispute, all the claims must be issued and heard individually.

9 VOCABULARY EXERCISE

Complete the sentences with the missing word or phrase (answers are at the back of the book):

1. The legal English term for monetary compensation is _____.

2. To _____ is the verb used to state that the claimant thinks or believes that the defendant committed a breach, but without it being proven in a court of law.

3. My client came to me in relation to a negligence claim. He wanted to issue proceedings immediately, but I advised him that first we need to send a _____ _____ _____ to the defendant stating the grounds of our claim.

4. The main purpose of the Civil Procedure Rules is known as the _____ _____. It is the spirit in which the parties should act in the proceedings.

5. The party that brings a claim is formally called a _____.

6. Counsel will be here in 15 minutes. Our solicitor will _____ her about the latest developments in the case before the hearing begins.

7. The defendant arrived at court without a legal representative. He conducted the hearing as a _____ __ _____.

8. The defendant was surprised to receive the claim form in the post. He

did not agree that he was in breach of contract and so decided to _____ the claim in full.

9. To _____ means to agree or accept that you are responsible for doing something, usually in a negative context.

10. During multi-track proceedings it is very common for the parties to make _____ to the court. These can be for specific reasons such as summary judgment, specific disclosure requests or to strike out the claim.

11. The _____ exercise is one of the most important parts of civil litigation proceedings. The Civil Procedure Rules state that all parties must states which documents they have in their possession.

12. The track which deals with higher value and more complicated claims is called the _____-_____.

13. An example of _____-_____ is the when defendant's lawyer asks questions to the claimant's witness.

14. In legal English, to be _____ means to be legally responsible for your acts or omissions.

15. After all parties have submitted their case to court, the judge will consider her _____ and will give judgment in the next two weeks.

16. The collocation used in legal English when the court gives damages to a claimant is to _____ damages.

17. It is a principle of English law that the claimant must _____ their loss. This means that they must try to keep their loss as low as reasonably possible.

18. If a married couple no longer wish to remain together, the legal collocation is that they _____ _____.

19. The legal term that means to "break" a contract is to _____.

20. Race, religion, age, sex, disability and sexual orientation are example of _____ claims.

10 PREPOSITION EXERCISE

Complete the sentences using the correct preposition (answers are at the back of the book):

1. The claimant issued a claim against the defendant ____ the grounds of nuisance.

2. To establish negligence under English law, there are a number of tests to satisfy. The first is to establish that the defendant owed the claimant a duty ____ care.

3. It is common for employees to bring ___ action for unfair dismissal against their ex-employers.

4. A claimant must issue a claim form with the court to start proceedings. If the facts or case are complicated, then the claimant can also file particulars ___ claim to set out the claim in detail.

5. One of the most important tasks for a claimant is to serve the claim form ___ the defendant.

6. If the defendant needs more time to respond to the claim then they can file an acknowledgement ___ service.

7. After receiving the claim form the defendant is given a limited amount of time in which to respond ____ the allegations made by the claimant.

8. It is common for the court to order a stay ____ proceedings. This means that the proceedings are stopped for a period of time.

9. In civil litigation, either a solicitor or a barrister may represent their client in court if they have rights of audience. If a solicitor wishes to use a barrister, they will draft a document called instructions ___ counsel. This document states what the solicitor is asking the barrister to do in the case.

10. After the defendant has served the defence on the claimant, the claimant has the right to reply ___ the defence. They have a limited period of time in which to do this.

11. The judge reserved judgment in the case. When he returned to court he found ____ favour of the claimant and awarded damages of £34,000.

12. Each statement of case that a party wishes to issue at court and serve on the other parties must contain a statement ___ truth.

13. The judge explained to the claimant that they must prove that the defendant is liable on the balance ___ probabilities.

14. An attachment ___ earnings order is when the court decide that the defendant must pay the debt in instalments every month from their salary to the claimant.

15. The court can order that any interest ___ the damages must also be paid by the defendant to the claimant.

16. The court found that the defendant was liable ____ breach of contract.

17. The most common civil litigation claim is an action in the tort ___ negligence.

18. The claimant thought that the goods were defective and so brought an action ____ product liability.

19. Battery and assault are type of trespass ___ the person.

20. I recently advised my client on a case about his neighbour trespassing ____ his property.

11 COLLOCATION EXERCISE

Complete the sentences using the correct collocation (answers are at the back of the book):

1. The newspaper reported that an allegation has been _____ against a local factory for nuisance. The claimant says that there is pollution coming from the factory and it is damaging the local environment.

2. An important principle of negligence is that any breach of a duty of care must _____ loss. There must be this connection between the breach and the loss.

3. If a potential defendant does not respond to a letter before action, the claimant may have no choice but to _____ a claim at their local county court.

4. In legal English the phrase to _____ to the court means to state an opinion to the court.

5. The legal English term that means to argue your case is to _____ your case to the court.

6. If a defendant states that they are not liable in any way, they _____ the allegations.

7. After a claimant has issued a claim against a defendant, the defendant has

a limited period of time to _____ to the claim.

8. The court will expect all parties to attend the final hearing. The court may _____ against a party if they are not at court.

9. The English legal system is designed to produce settlements in cases. It is common for either party to _____ a Part 36 offer during the proceedings in order to settle the claim.

10. It is usual for a solicitor to brief a barrister before a _____ or a trial to make sure they are up to date with all developments in the case.

11. When a defendant or the defendant's advocate asks questions to the defendant about the case in court, the legal term is _____-___-_____.

12. After the court has heard all the evidence, the judge will _____ judgment.

13. If the losing party feels that the judgment of the court is incorrect, they can ask the court to _____ them _____ to appeal.

14. After the judge has read the judgment to the court, they will _____ an order. This means that they will officially state what the losing party has to do (for example, pay damages to the claimant, pay costs, comply with an injunction, etc).

15. One remedy for a claimant is to ask the court to _____ a contract. This means that the court will put the parties back in the position they were in, if the contract had never existed.

16. My neighbour always parks his car on my property. I will go to court and seek an _____ for him to stop.

17. It's so unfair that I had to pay for expensive lawyers to get my money from the defendant. I will _____ an order for costs from the court so he has to pay my legal fees.

18. The company lost a lot of money last year and so they _____ bankrupt after making an application to the court.

19. Some defendants do not pay their judgment debts on time, accordingly, bailiffs are sometimes employed by the court to _____ these judgments.

20. During proceedings, the court will _____ directions to the parties so that they know what they have to do and when to do it.

12 REPLACE THE INCORRECT WORD

Find and replace the incorrect word with the correct one (answers are at the back of the book):

1. The rules that govern civil litigation in England and Wales are known as the Common Procedure Rules.

2. If a defendant fails to file a defence or an acknowledgment of service on time, then the claimant can apply to the court for a summary judgment.

3. Both parties can attempt to resolve their dispute away from the court by organising Alternative Disagreement Resolution.

4. The person who repossesses property to pay for a judgment debt is known as Recorder.

5. If there are many claimants and/or many defendants, the court may order that the claims are heard together. This is known as a Group Proceedings Order.

6. The tort of interfering with another person's property or land is known as nuisance.

7. The tort of stopping someone from quietly enjoying their own property or land is known as trespass.

8. If all the parties agree to settle the case, in legal English it is said that the matter has been dissolved.

9. A defendant has three choices when they receive a claim form. They can accept the claim, deny the claim or file an acknowledgment of service.

10. The fastest and easiest route in the Civil Procedure Rules is called the small claims track. This is for low value, simple claims.

11. Usually a claim will have a claimant and a defendant. If there is another party to the proceedings who have an interest in the claim, they are called an extra party.

12. At the beginning of some hearings, the claimant and the defendant will be able to give an initial statement to the court, explaining their position in the case.

13. The judge may delay handing down their judgment to the parties. This gives them more time to consider their verdict. The legal English phrase used is to "withhold judgment".

14. It is possible for more than one person to be liable for a tort and for a group of people to be liable together. In this situation the phrase joint and separate liability can be used.

15. My friend James sold me a car last week. He said it was in good condition and didn't have any accidents. Later I discovered this was not true and so I am suing James for negligence.

16. Another company copied my friend's book without her permission. She has issued proceedings against them for copyright breach.

17. When a company does not have enough money to pay its creditors, specific proceedings called bankruptcy proceedings can be brought against the company.

18. A witness demand is a court order that requires a witness to attend court or provide evidence.

19. The procedure for distributing the assets of a person who has just died is called defamation.

20. If a defendant believes that a claim is brought that has little or no chance of success, they can make an application to the court for default judgment.

13 ANSWERS

True or False:

1. True

2. True

3. False

4. True

5. False

6. False

7. False

8. True

9. True

10. False

11. True

12. True

13. False

14. True

15. False

16. True

17. False

18. False

19. True

20. False

Vocabulary Exercise:

1. damages

2. allege

3. letter before action

4. overriding objective

5. claimant

6. brief

7. litigant in person

8. defend/deny

9. admit

10. applications

11. disclosure

12. multi-track

13. cross-examine

14. liable

15. verdict

16. award

17. mitigate

18. get divorced

19. breach

20. discrimination

Prepositions Exercise:

1. on

2. of

3. an

4. of

5. on

6. of

7. to

8. of

9. to

10. to

11. in

12. of

13. of

14. of

15. on

16. for

17. of

18. for

19. to

20. on

Collocations Exercise:

1. made

2. cause

3. issue

4. submit

5. plead

6. deny

7. respond

8. find

9. make

10. hearing

11. examination-in-chief

12. give

13. grant/leave

14. make

15. rescind

16. injunction

17. seek

18. went

19. enforce

20. give

Replace the Incorrect Word

1. ~~Common~~, Civil

2. ~~summary~~, default

3. ~~Disagreement~~, Dispute

4. ~~Recorder~~, Bailiff

5. ~~Proceedings~~, Litigation

6. ~~nuisance~~, trespass

7. ~~trespass~~, nuisance

8. ~~dissolved~~, resolved

9. ~~accept~~, admit

10. ~~Track~~, Court

11. ~~Extra~~, Third

12. ~~initial~~, opening

13. ~~withhold~~, reserve

14. ~~separate~~, several

15. ~~negligence~~, misrepresentation

16. ~~breach~~, infringement

17. ~~bankruptcy~~, insolvency

18. ~~demand~~, summons

19. ~~defamation~~, wills and probate

20. ~~default~~, summary

ABOUT THE AUTHOR

Michael Howard is a solicitor and legal English lecturer from London. He grew up in Surrey, England and qualified as a solicitor in 2005. After many years of legal practice he decided to travel around Europe and the Middle East lecturing law and teaching English. His travels took him to Poland, Germany, Dubai, Abu Dhabi and finally back to the UK where he was invited to teach legal English to foreign lawyers and law students at courses run at Cambridge University. Michael now works in legal publishing and spends his free time writing vocabulary and study packs to help foreign lawyers improve their legal English. In April 2013 he published his first set of books on the English Legal System and in November 2013 he followed this up with Civil Litigation and Dispute Resolution. The most recent set in his catalogue is entitled Drafting Commercial Contracts. Alongside writing and publishing he spends time with his family and friends in South London and playing the guitar. His vocabulary series and study packs are all available on Amazon on Kindle and in paperback.

Printed in Great Britain
by Amazon

59941950R00058